EXTRAORDINARY
LESSONS
FROM AN
ORDINARY LIFE

Simple Insights
for a Better Life

by Mike Jaroch

Proudly Published in the USA by
Thornton Publishing, Inc
17011 Lincoln Ave. #408
Parker, CO 80134

Phone: (303)-794-8888
Fax: (720)-863-2013

BooksToBelieveIn.com
publisher@bookstobelievein.com

ISBN: 1530611385

Best Wishes, Always!

Mike Jarvis

May, 2017

*Mike with his "pride and joy", all five of his grandsons,
at his condo on Hilton Head Island (The Island Club complex).*

*The boys are trying on their life jackets before an
exciting ride around the island on the boat
of long-time friend, Frank Russo.*

*From left to right are Brian Martin, twins Ryan and Luke
Jaroch, Joseph Martin, and oldest grandson, Sam Jaroch.*

Dedicated to those
who have improved my
life and work...

and to my
five grandsons.

TABLE OF CONTENTS

Money equals choices not things: *To achieve the type of financial freedom that few know, focus on the options money gives you.*

Persistence as the ultimate attribute: *The famous quote of President Calvin Coolidge made so much sense and immediately became my favorite.*

Nobody can ring your bell: *The intimidators in life move on to prey on others when they realize they can't ring your bell.*

When things aren't going your way - They are: *Today's rejections, no matter how painful, are tomorrow's opportunities.*

Hone your patience to best your competition: *With your eyes always on the prize, the ability to outwait everyone, if need be, is so important.*

Create a dilemma: *Rather than wait for that special wish to happen make the goal that of causing many to happen at once.*

Give me the ball: *When the pressure was on to win the game, the great basketball player, Larry Bird, wanted the ball to come to him.*

Make an early savings deposit: *A mental game I played on myself to be more like my mentor. It set me free to take risks and step forward as never before.*

No decision is a decision: *The illusion of buying more time actually takes it away leaving at best a hurried decision process or at worst panic.*

80 percent of success is just showing up: *When Woody Allen s insight becomes a part of you, your only remaining fear is to hesitate.*

Focus: *Developing your A-list of priorities is one thing. What differentiates you is having the discipline to focus on the most critical things.*

Go to the pain: *The Horse Whisperer taught me how moving counter to our intuition creates an advantage in people relations.*

Begin at the end: *Whether the news is good or bad, it's easier to begin there and cover the context later.*

Management makes 'the' difference: *Results, positive or negative, are the leader's problem. Excellent leaders know their reaction makes the difference.*

Be obsessive about communication: *Despite all the wonders of technology, unresponsive is the norm. Communicate, Respond, and Stand Out!*

The word is integrity: *Your word is your bond. You do as you say and nothing less. A leader without integrity is dead in place.*

Trusting your own judgment: *My student became my teacher when he asked the impossible question.*

Further reflections to share

Acknowledgements

About the Author - Mike Jaroch

Other books by Mike Jaroch

Resources

FOREWORD

The Greatest Discovery Of Any Generation Is That A Human Being Can Alter His Life By Altering His Attitude.
- William James

These lessons represent the path of my life that I found, observed, and learned along the way. Some I've carried with me for decades. How they came to be was never part of an overt plan. I have simply used them so I could remember the stories and insights behind them. I repeated them often to myself and to friends and colleagues as a way of keeping a clear focus on the road ahead. They have helped me to stay strong and determined on what I found important in building a life well lived, with family and a successful career at the heart of it. Much to my surprise, I began to overhear others reference these lessons, such as, "you know what Mike says, you have to go to the pain."

This compelled me to write these stories down, so they might inspire ordinary people (like me) living ordinary lives (like mine). In writing these stories, I began to see them as a guiding roadmap for my grandsons. We can get caught up in big achievements, which at best come along sporadically. I believe our everyday experiences are just as important. The everyday experiences can teach us extraordinary lessons, truths really, that can forever affect our lives. I found through the years that these stories grounded me and I wish something like that for my grandsons. The glitz and glamour touted by the cult of celebrity serve only to distract us from the importance of our own lives. I hope everyone, my grandsons most especially, realizes that their lives may become extraordinary in their own right.

I am honored and humbled that you would take some of your busy time to spend with me as I tell about my life of lessons. Thank you so very much.

~*Mike Jaroch*

You Are What You Think About

A door-to-door salesman taught me one of the most important lessons of life. The most brutal truth.

After I graduated from high school, I worked for 14 months on the shipping docks at a picture frame manufacturer to earn money for college. The factory was just four blocks from my home, so on most days I dashed home for lunch with my mom.

One day, I arrived home soaked to the skin, having run through a heavy downpour. I was very surprised to find my mother reviewing an order with the door-to-door salesman. Incredulous, I asked him, 'Why would you go door-to-door on such a wet, miserable day?'

What he told me, as I quickly ate my sandwich, opened my eyes to a basic insight on the real world. He pointed out to the rain and told me that whenever he woke up to a miserable day of rain or snow he got excited. He knew he would sell much more of his products. Why? All his buyers, mainly housewives, would be at home! It made sense to me immediately: Tough to sell much going door-to-door when no one is home.

He recognized my reaction with a smile. Mine was the typical reaction of other sales people. When they saw rain, they only thought of walking through the rain. With that outlook, it would be better to go back to bed and wait for the sun to come out.

On the surface this is a lesson in the proverbial glass that one can choose to see as half-full or half-empty. Beneath that, he avoided letting things beyond his control victimize him. The way he did this gave him an edge over his competition. His positive thinking led to positive outcomes. Since that day, I've emulated that salesman, his positive attitude, and his belief that you are what you think about.

I began watching people and how their attitudes shaped their days. Throughout my time in college, I worked in the dish rooms of various dormitories. I not only made much needed extra money, but I also got to enjoy free meals.

At the end of a semester in my sophomore year, as I was about to leave the cleaning room, my supervisor called me into his office. He told me something that he had observed. When I came to work in a good mood the entire crew would be in a good mood. On the occasional days when I was down, the entire crew would be down.

He wanted me to know the impact and influence my attitude had on others. I'm sure I didn't fully appreciate what he said on that particular day as much as its importance struck me as the years went by.

I came to see how the pessimists create their own self-fulfilling prophesies. A person's attitude shapes their potential. I learned to put as much distance as possible between myself and a pessimist. In the end, it comes back to my friend the door-to-door salesman and the realization that attitude is, indeed, the magic word.

*The entire Jaroch clan of 13 children taken
behind their home in Mundelein, IL. approximately 1965.
Mike is pictured on the far left holding
the youngest child, Christopher.*

KNOWING THE
RIGHT MOMENT

A short article by Winston Churchill during a rest break on the shipping dock taught me the importance of timing.

Coming from a family of thirteen children, we always knew that if we were to go to college we would have to work that out on our own. After all, in a family of that many, you had to make your presence known and keep on your toes. I earned my initial funds for school by working on the shipping docks of the manufacturing plant.

My first day on the job, I met Art who had the same plan as I did. He was one year ahead of me in school and just finishing his first year at the factory. Right away, he asked me if I had told the bosses of my plan to enroll in college the following year. Of course

I told them, assuming they would see that as admirable. I understood that it was a key to my getting the job.

Art told me that I had made a big mistake by telling them of my plans. He had done the same a year earlier and, with the company knowing he was not there for long, he had never been given a raise. Upon his departure, since we planned to attend the same school, we promised to connect the next year.

Shortly after he left, during a work break on the docks, I read an article by Winston Churchill. The great leader shared his thoughts on "knowing the right moment" and the importance of refining your sense of timing. I took it to heart and tried it out.

When my first supervisor, Bernie, got promoted and sent to California to open a new plant, I saw my "moment." At his celebration party, I asked for a pay raise and received it immediately.

Then came the replacement, Orville. He wasn't well received by the department and, over his first few months, some of the better employees quit or managed a transfer out of our area. I could see how this bothered him. I let him know that he could count on me given my mission to earn money to go to college. I kept my word, and eventually when I asked him for a raise I received a generous one.

Sometimes, it's just luck, but you shouldn't let that stop you. When I joined the company bowling league, I ended up on a team with the CEO. We got to know each other, our team did well, and along the way the next pay raise came. Finally, one weekend, I volunteered to move furniture in the executive suite. I hit it off with the VP of Sales and you can guess what came next.

In all, by the time I left for college, I had received six pay increases. I couldn't wait to bump into Art! Yet, I feel more important than the pay increases was the reward for developing my sense of timing. You have to work hard, hold on to your attitude, and wait for the opening. Then, make your move. Eventually, it became instinctive for me and has been invaluable for me throughout my life.

Mike's senior class picture.
Mundelein High School - 1962

BE HONEST WITH YOURSELF ABOUT YOURSELF

I took up the sport of golf and the first important lesson I learned had nothing to do with hitting the ball.

I have often said that my short time on the shipping docks is where I actually earned my first college degree. Certainly, it was the centerpiece of my education; less formal but no less important. While packing boxes and loading and unloading the delivery trucks, I learned many things from the laborers and drivers, including the common sense of business logic and how to get from point A to point B in a straight line.

Many of the lessons in life and business come in just this way, from those around you, whether at work or at play. In a specific instance, I joined the factory golf league to try my hand at Arnold Palmer's sport. He was the king and he made it look fun. Like a lot of us, I wanted to be as good as him. The first time I stepped onto a golf course I was absolutely smitten by the beauty of the place. I was transported away from the troubles of the day to a place of peace and tranquility. Golf has been my passion ever since that day.

Before my very first match, I heard about Howie, who was in my foursome. Many of the other players went out of their way to warn me about him. He had a reputation for cheating on his score and he lived up to this quite quickly. I can still see his first few drives slicing out of bounds and by the time he had putted out on the first hole he might have had ten strokes for all I knew. When we each called out our score, Howie said, "Give me bogey 5." So it went for the entire nine holes.

Like the others, I started counting his strokes, and it was unbelievable, both what he reported as his score and his lack of sportsmanship. The others were so used to this that they simply put down the correct score no matter what he said. They had given up on correcting him.

It was all very interesting to me, but not just his cheating as much as his self deception. He seemed totally convinced about his score, obliviously and without doubt. I was intrigued: A person could so flagrantly deceive oneself about one's performance, abilities, and capabilities.

In the clubhouse afterwards, people were shaking their heads and chuckling about Howie's scores. But what Howie showed me is that we were each capable of self-deception at some degree. Who is to say that I wasn't acting the same way elsewhere in my life? I silently vowed to be honest with myself about my ways.

Now having said this, I know it's impossible to achieve 100 percent objectivity. The competition of life is tough and sometimes, it seems to me, having a few illusions about one's abilities may just help you cope. Further to the point, being an optimist shouldn't separate you from being a realist.

In any case, strive to be honest, brutally honest, about the person you see in the mirror each morning. Keep an accurate life score.

Mike's grammar school graduation picture.
Santa Maria del Popolo grade school,
Mundelein, IL., 1958

FOR ANYTHING TO BE TOTALLY SPONTANEOUS, IT MUST BE REHEARSED

My professor said something strange and also very important.

It was just an elective Education class to pick up a few required semester hours. But, I learned an important lesson about how I was "built to communicate" and how that was dependent on preparation.

I'm an informal person. I prefer to engage people in a conversation versus presenting to people. Being informal seems at first glance to mean acting without a plan. Isn't that what we see on stage? We may tend to think that the people who are great on stage are naturals at casually and comfortably communicating in front of people. Not true.

To the professor's point: Prepare yourself so well that your 'presentation' seems very informal, spontaneous, off the top of your head. In fact, it's not at all. Instead you have studied and rehearsed so well that you can effectively have meaningful and heartfelt conversations with others, whether it's one person or 10,000 people. Just remember what the professor said.

Money Equals Choices Not Things

To achieve the type of financial freedom that few know, focus on the options money gives you.

When you come from a big family and have to make your way without much financial help from others, the allure is to treat yourself to all the goodies in life. We can become hypnotized by want of luxury.

But money can be viewed a different way. I learned a lesson early on about how to use money, one that isn't often promoted. At my first job out of college, Tim Ames changed my perspective on the great advantage of achieving a level of financial independence. One day, I asked him what he did for a living.

'I spend a few hours each day managing investments and then devote much of my time to my aging parents and love of golf,' he said. Tim was well to do and yet you couldn't see it in the car he drove, the clothes he wore, or his home.

I had the youthful nerve to comment, 'That must be a lot of money.'

He told me, 'I suppose so, if a million or more dollars can be considered large.'

Of course, I was blown away. It didn't make sense. I just had to ask, 'Why don't you act like you have that much money?'

He told me the unspoken advantage of wealth: Money equals freedom, not things. He enjoyed his freedom and much preferred his choices in life over surrounding himself with objects.

Thanks to Tim, I set a new course in life, and developed this discipline. Once I experienced it, I became convinced that there is absolutely NO substitute for living with such freedom.

PERSISTENCE AS THE ULTIMATE ATTRIBUTE

The famous quote of President Calvin Coolidge made so much sense and immediately became my favorite.

When you don't have some of the advantages of others, it's reassuring that your own determination, the one element over which you have absolute control, is such a great equalizer. In fact, it actually wins the day.

As you might imagine, I am a person who loves a meaningful quote and have used them to motivate and guide myself throughout my life. My favorite quote is PERSISTENCE by President Calvin Coolidge.

Nothing in the world can take the place of Persistence.

Talent will not; nothing is more common than unsuccessful men with talent.

Genius will not; unrewarded genius is almost a proverb.

Education will not; the world is full of educated derelicts.

Persistence and determination alone are omnipotent.

Life is an equal opportunity test. Everyone gets knocked down, kicked in the face, suffers setbacks and even tragedies, no matter their status and station in life. What separates us as individuals is the ability to pick yourself up off the floor, dust yourself off, shake off the setbacks, and carry on, ever persistent and determined to climb the hill of life. I am sure that your life, like mine, has many key moments when your determination made all the difference in success versus failure.

In one instance, I was preparing for a rigorous four-hour psychological exam as the final step in applying for my first full-time job. A lot was at stake. I wanted the job, yes, but also I needed the job, having found out a few weeks earlier that my wife of five months was expecting our first child. To be interviewed by a "shrink" was a little unnerving, to say the least. Shortly before leaving the house to catch the morning train into downtown Chicago, I thumbed through the morning newspaper and saw a headline: Tim Ames was dead in a car accident.

I remember falling back onto our couch, stunned. Even now, as I write, those feelings overwhelm me. I thought, What's the use in trying? You work so hard to make it, and then something like this happens! Why bother even catching the train? How can I be upbeat on this interview now?

I knew, of course, Tim would be so very disappointed with me if his death, tragic as it was, would be an excuse for not persisting, for losing my determination.

I asked myself, what if I'm just lucky enough to live to be 60 years old and what will I have to show for it? I caught the train, spent that hour talking to myself, doing my best to be positive. The interview went well, I got the job, and my career began in earnest. Thank you and God bless you, Tim Ames.

*Mike and his wife, Marsha, on their wedding day,
June 24, 1967. Mike's parents, Stan and Jayne Jaroch
are pictured on the church steps with them.*

Nobody Can Ring Your Bell

The intimidators in life move on to prey on others when they realize they can't ring your bell.

Funny how sometimes life prepares you for something when you don't even realize it's happening. So it was with this lesson. Years ago, a book, Winning Through Intimidation, made a big impact. I read it and found it interesting. Not that I was planning on becoming a master of intimidation; but, it made me aware of the fact that some folks just love to intimidate you. Whatever their methods and manner, the desired result was the same - put you in a corner, on the defensive and begging for mercy.

Well, as fate would have it, I began a job with a new company shortly after reading the book.

Throughout the interviewing and orientation process, folks warned me about Stu, a department head in the plant where I would be Personnel Manager. By my first day on the job, I was practically having nightmares about the dreaded Stu.

Fortunately, I went back to the book and refreshed my memory about the techniques of intimidation. Armed with that support, within hours of being on the job, I called Stu and asked him to give me a tour of his area of the plant and then suggested we have lunch afterwards in the plant cafeteria.

I went straight at him, so to speak, not most people's way with him. It was amazingly easy to disarm him and we actually became good friends. The lesson was clear to me. Don't give those who would try to intimidate you the pleasure and watch how quickly they move on to others. It's no fun when they can't ring your bell.

WHEN THINGS AREN'T GOING YOUR WAY - THEY ARE

Today's rejections, no matter how painful, are tomorrow's opportunities.

No matter how smart you are, you never really know how things will finally conclude. It's pretty easy to get attached to what is right, important, and necessary for you to get what you want and be happy. When things go against your ideas, your goals and objectives, it can be hard to see it otherwise. At these times, however, it's good to check in on the bigger picture and stay focused on what is important. Remember, you are most of the time in midstream and you don't know how it will ultimately turn out.

I have certainly had my fair share of rejections and disappointments. Two that come to the forefront and clearly made this lesson come to life for me, I will relate to you. With the first situation I'll mention, it took a few years before this lesson came home to me.

With the second, the lesson was immediate and overwhelming.

I was about twelve years into my business career when a fantastic job opportunity presented itself. My manager was promoted to the corporate office and his management position at our multi-facility site was therefore available. I wanted that job so badly. I had prepared myself for it, and most everyone said I was all but assured of getting the promotion.

I did not get the job. My boss picked another fellow who was much more of his friend and golf buddy. I was devastated at the time and when, a few months later, I was offered another position as a consolation prize I left that location and moved on.

As fate would have it, two years later I was asked to go back and take over that position due to senior management's unhappiness with results there. So in the end I got the job I wanted, did very well, and my career took off from there.

As for the other situation, back in the late 1970s and early 1980s, I created and co-authored with some of my brothers a series of children's books. We were excited about their potential for success and I tried every marketing strategy possible to promote and sell the books.

One year, I wanted desperately to attend the annual bookseller's convention to be held in Los Angeles, California. I could not afford to pay for such a trip and our publisher was unwilling to cover my costs to join the group attending. I was very disappointed, particularly since they intended to display our books prominently and promote them heavily.

Oh so tragically, the plane I would have been on crashed upon takeoff from O'Hare airport in Chicago. When I heard the news and realized it was the flight I wanted to be on, this lesson was forever imprinted upon me. Please, keep your perspective and have an unabiding faith knowing that things are indeed going your way.

Mike at work in Springfield, IL., the state capital, with Representative Robert W. Churchill. Mike was very involved in both local and state politics in Illinois for several years.

HONE YOUR PATIENCE
TO BEST THE COMPETITION

With your eyes always on the prize, the ability to outwait everyone, if need be, is so important.

Maybe because the competition to win is so fierce, we get over-anxious to make something happen. Adopting the discipline of patience as a key strategy can make the difference between success and failure.

I think of the playing of sports, or a game like chess, as great teachers of this lesson. With my eyes always on the goal, I will wait and wait and wait, if that's what it takes to let the situation develop. If you know exactly what you are looking for, the path to success will take shape, and a better sense of the right time will reveal itself.

You need a lot of tools in your tool chest to negotiate life on your terms. To have both the nerve to show up and the discipline of patience to perfect your timing is a powerful combination. Think about it and work on it, knowing that we all spend some time "behind the dark side of moon" during our lives. Patience brings us back around and into the light of day.

CREATE A DILEMMA

Rather than wait for that special wish to happen make the goal that of causing many to happen at once.

The genesis of this lesson came from my own job seeking experiences and those of others I observed. Simply put, you have the great interview for the job you most covet, and then place yourself on hold, waiting for the offer to arrive. Weeks might go by, and in the end you are told that someone else got the job. Not only are you devastated with a sinking morale, you've lost weeks of momentum towards other possibilities and opportunities.

My answer to this situation is "create a dilemma," that is, create a serious logjam of possibilities. It was born as a way of motivating myself and others to intentionally put yourself in a desirable position. I came to realize that achieving such a level of conflicts is itself the goal that ultimately leads to success.

Mike, Marsha, with daughter, Julie and husband Mike Martin, with grandson Brian Martin, along with son, Mike and wife Jennifer, with grandson Sam Jaroch. Enjoying time together on their favorite place to escape, Hilton Head Island, South Carolina.

GIVE ME THE BALL

When the pressure was on to win the game, the great basketball player, Larry Bird, wanted the ball to come to him.

I have always admired Larry Bird. Watching him play basketball, with such talent in every aspect of the game, was such a joy. When a game was on the line in the closing seconds, he would insist that the play be drawn up so he got the final shot, win or lose.

When I heard this, it struck me that most of us might hope that the ball didn't end up in our hands for that final shot. Win or lose, alone, seems a burden to avoid not accept. Larry taught us to accept such a responsibility, proactively ask for it, embrace it, and want it as desperately as victory itself.

I love the expression "Leave it on the Field!" Makes no sense to save some of your effort for when the competition is over.

Son, Mike, and daughter, Julie, with Mike at his MBA graduation event at the Lake Forest Graduate School of Management, Lake Forest, Ill. June, 1985.

Make An Early Savings Deposit

A mental game I played on myself to be more like my mentor. It set me free to take risks and step forward as never before.

First and foremost, you will be far more successful if you actively recruit mentors. I have been fortunate to have a number of outstanding mentors and supporters as I've made my way through life. Thankfully, they saw something in me that made it worth their time to invest in my development. I have tried my best to do the same for many of the hard working ambitious young people I've been fortunate to meet.

As for my mentors, a few clearly stand out and will be remembered always. One of those was a high-ranking executive with Baxter Healthcare, Steve Lazarus. Our careers intersected numerous times over the years and each time he was more than a colleague, boss, or friend.

Even before we came to know each other, Steve inadvertently taught me a life lesson. Interestingly, my thought that led to the lesson was actually quite wrongheaded, silly really, but it served a purpose nonetheless.

Steve could mesmerize a large audience for an hour or two, always without any notes. I wondered what would give someone such a level of confidence enabling him to perform so eloquently. If only I had his salary, his level of financial success, I, too, would have such confidence.

As I say, it's a silly idea to think that Steve's ability and immense intelligence had to do with his income. Nevertheless, as a young manager with a family, that's the connection I made. Fortunately, I made something of that mistaken insight. I asked myself, how would I perform if I had a million dollars in the bank?

Ask yourself that and then start acting accordingly. Right now. That is what I did. I mentally made a deposit and changed my behavior. From that very day to the present, I took on a level of confidence and willingness to take risks that I never could have imagined.

No Decision
IS A Decision

The illusion of buying more time actually takes it away leaving at best a hurried decision process or at worst panic.

I have been blessed to have gained my independence these past twelve years as a management consultant. Certainly, my work as a consultant has allowed me a multitude of opportunities to apply, instruct, and educate on my life of lessons. A day in the life of an executive leader consists of such a wide variety of decisions that it's hard to keep up. That I am allowed to assist with some of those decisions has been and continues to be an honor for me.

I embrace my being called their "chief tenacity officer," helping to drive execution on a long list of critical issues. When you avoid making a decision, the delay or failure to act, is in fact a decision in and of itself.

This is being written during very difficult economic times when many companies are faced with very difficult decisions affecting the lives of their employees. Major decisions such as facility closings and staff reductions are being dealt with daily. You can see where executives who decide not to decide face more difficult and complex decisions weeks or months later.

Yes, it can be a fine line between using the strategy of having patience and the unwillingness to make a clear decision and act. The true genius of a great leader is understanding the difference.

When we realize the vital importance of this, it's amazing how decisive we can become and by doing so we acquire a trait that no leader can survive without.

As a side note, I have come to use what I call "thinking along the spectrum" as a decision making technique. Simply put, lay out both extreme ends of the spectrum of the decision you face. This clarifies the parameters. Then, assuming neither extreme makes sense, you can begin to narrow the decision possibilities by working your way in along the spectrum. By setting parameters and then ruling out the impossible, you can then act with more confidence on the correct decision.

80 PERCENT OF SUCCESS IS JUST SHOWING UP

When Woody Allen's insight becomes a part of you, your only remaining fear is to hesitate.

Enter one, Rick Adam, into my life of lessons. I could devote an entire chapter on the significant and wonderful impact that Rick Adam had on both my personal and professional lives.

For my purposes here, I must mention at least two of the more important lessons that came to me through my relationship with Rick. First, Rick introduced me to Woody Allen's famous quote, "80 percent of success is just showing up." For Rick, it was not just a casual reference. This quote had become a way of life, a standard operating procedure, so to say.

While most folks hesitate to take action until they are well prepared, if not overly prepared, they lose out to those who aren't afraid to just show up. It reminds me of Nike's great slogan, "Just Do It." Ultimately, it eliminated all insecurities of being unprepared, feeling awkward, being rejected, etc. By eliminating those, it reverses the fear, which becomes a compulsion to act. The only real fear is that I will miss an opportunity because I hesitated.

Eventually, as for Rick, this quote became a part of me, an essential part of me, and has reaped many rewards for me. Being a risk taker comes naturally. I like to think this trait has rubbed off on my children and is beginning to get imparted to my grandsons. My oldest grandson, Sam, is fond of telling people "I'm a risk taker like my Grandpa."

FOCUS

*Mike with his long-time golf buddies of over 30 years.
They began together in Illinois and now live in four
different states. However, they have met every
year for the past 20 years to play four rounds
of very competitive golf. From left to right,
Bill, Lenny, Mike, and Geoff.*

Developing your A-list of priorities is one thing. What differentiates you is having the discipline to focus on the most critical things.

I call Rick a teacher, though many times, the term "taskmaster" might actually be more appropriate. Simply put, this lesson is about having the self discipline to focus on the most important, critical issues and take action on priorities.

A-list items may not include things we like to do. You have the awareness and honesty to know the most critical aspects of your job. Now, keep the commitment to address them, first and foremost. The famous management expert, Peter Drucker, would say when you complete that handful of items on the A-list you don't move to the B-list. Instead, you create a new A-list.

Rick, by preaching about the A-list items and holding his team accountable to them, taught me the importance of focusing in such a manner and showed me what a difference this makes in success across all areas of life.

GO TO THE PAIN

The Horse Whisperer taught me how moving counter to our intuition creates an advantage in people relations.

There I was, performing the great art of channel surfing with the remote control, as guys are want to do. Up came a picture of a fellow poking a horse in the side. I stopped long enough to see what that was all about. The point of the clip was how the horse reacted to it.

It was a PBS program on the famous horse trainer, Monty Roberts, the "horse whisperer" as he is known for his training methods. At that moment, he was demonstrating how horses "turn to the pain" versus humans who "turn away from the pain." As he poked the horse in the side, the horse turned his head around towards Monty. He moved around the horse and poked him in his other side and again the horse turned his head toward his trainer.

At that moment, it struck me that there was an important lesson there for human relations - go to the pain. Certainly no one likes pain, conflict, difficulties; but, if one can learn to go to the pain points versus avoiding, delaying, and turning away from them, things may actually be easier to deal with successfully. One needs only to have the courage to go there, that place where the majority of people will not.

For me, it started with having the conversation I least wanted to have, meeting with the person I least wanted to meet with, returning the phone call first that I least wanted to have. Over time, it became a natural way of behaving for me. It has clearly become one of my favorite axioms in coaching others.

BEGIN AT THE END

Mike on the right at a wedding event in New York City with his two older brothers, Stan(seated) and Tim.

Whether the news is good or bad, it's easier to begin there and cover the context later.

Ever talk to someone about your performance, something you've done or haven't done, and you wonder if they are praising you or condemning you? You wait, anxiously, for them to deliver their point, the punch line, or the final verdict - guilty or not guilty. Believe me, they are wishing they could find it, too.

In the profession of human resources, we are often called upon to have those conversations no one else wants to have, many of which are very sensitive and multilayered. I came to the conclusion that it was so much easier and less stressful if I began at the end, the news headline. With the decision known and on the table, I slowly revealed the details and the context.

Leaders who are unwilling to have such conversations appreciate how much easier the conversation is when they state the conclusion directly. This lesson is embedded in the well-known speech outline: tell the audience what you are going to say, say it, and tell them what you said.

Management Makes 'THE' Difference

Results, positive or negative, are the leader's problem. Excellent leaders know their reaction makes 'the' difference.

When you are the leader, you face a million and one problems. Often, not one of them is your fault. How you handle them makes or breaks your team or company. What do you do?

If you have ever experienced poor leadership you can discern between whether your leader makes 'a' difference and 'the' difference. It's no wonder so much has been said about the vital role of management.

In my work with both great leaders and poor ones, I focus on that one little word called an article, a or the. The importance and impact of their leadership lies in which word you use and that you emphasize it.

Management makes a difference.

or

Management makes **the** difference.

If you are the leader those million and one problems are your problems. The buck truly does stop with you.

Whether you are a leader of many or a leader of one, when you are tempted to pawn off the problem on others, remember you and everyone watching you will know 'the' difference.

BE OBSESSIVE
ABOUT COMMUNICATION

Mike walking Julie down the aisle at her wedding in June, 2001. The wedding was a most memorable event held in Marietta, GA.

Despite all the wonders of technology, unresponsive is the

norm. Communicate, Respond, and Stand Out!

Does a day go by anymore where the lack of responsiveness and untimely communication doesn't hit us in the face? We have instant communication in any number of ways around the world and yet sometimes the Pony Express looks attractive for some people.

I am fond of saying that no one "out communicates" me. I don't sit on phone messages, emails, etc. I pride myself on how well I communicate and stay in touch. Early in my career, I never left the office without all my phone messages returned. Later, especially these last dozen years as an independent consultant, my obsession with being on top of all communications differentiates me and my practice.

With unresponsiveness now the norm what an absolute easy way to standout from the pack and be seen in a different and special light. Communicate, early and often!

THE WORD
IS INTEGRITY

Your word is your bond. You do as you say and nothing less. A leader without integrity is dead in place.

There is a wonderful and dramatic story told about a prisoner of war during the Vietnam War. He was held several years before his release and for many of those years he tried desperately to get a message out to his young son back in the United States.

Finally, somehow, he found a way to get his message to his boy. Amazingly, his message was so simple, so brief, and yet so profound. It read as follows - "The word is INTEGRITY" That was it, that was what he so desperately wanted to tell his son, what he wanted him to know above all else to guide him through his life.

Stunning isn't it? The dictionary describes integrity as a quality or state of being complete or undivided; soundness and incorruptible; a firm adherence to a code of values. How about Wikipedia on the meaning of integrity? The honesty and truthfulness of one's actions; the opposite of hypocrisy; consistency of character; acting according to the beliefs and principles you claim to hold.

I synthesize this simply: Be a person of your word. Your word is your bond. People can totally trust what you say you will do; you deliver as promised and people can completely rely on you to do so.

I am fond of saying that integrity is all a leader really has to work with. Without it they are "dead in place" and probably don't know it. Without integrity you lose trust. Take away trust and you stop the free flow of timely, unfiltered information. Information is a leader's lifeblood, without it he or she can't make effective decisions. If they don't have integrity, they aren't leaders.

For all of you not in formal leadership positions, you will find with integrity you can gain much respect, informal authority, and a high level of influence.

TRUSTING YOUR OWN JUDGMENT

My student became my teacher when he asked the impossible question.

As you can see, if you keep your eyes open, your life can be fulfilled with special learning moments. The key is to see and understand those moments for what they are, capture them, document them, internalize them and make them part of your being, maybe even the essence of who you are.

I have had the honor of being an Adjunct Professor at the University of Denver and did my part to bring real world experience and lessons into my classroom. After a class one night, one of my students, Charlie, was very patient as I finished up a number of conversations with other students. When he finally had my full attention, I told him I admired his patience in waiting to see me. He said he wanted to be alone with me when he asked his "very important" question.

"What was the single most important lesson that you have learned in your career of 40 some years?" he asked.

How could anyone possibly answer such a question? Yet, in the very next moment, I knew the answer precisely. I gave it to him on the condition he would share it with others, which he promised he would do.

My single, most important lesson was this: Learning to trust my own instincts and judgment. The sooner a person reaches that level of self-trust, the sooner all good things would happen for him or her.

Thank you, Charlie, wherever you may be in your career, for bringing forth such a strong and real truth for me to share with you and many others since that evening in an empty classroom.

FURTHER REFLECTIONS
TO SHARE

**Life
is**

*Mike celebrating his 40ᵗʰ birthday at a surprise party
held for him by family, friends, and associates
at Baxter Healthcare Corp. in Illinois.*

about
Quality not Quantity

Yes, we might all like to live for a very long time. In the end, you may have little to say about how long you are blessed to be here. So put the focus on what you make of your life. You have everything to say about that!

Self-Reliance

Of all the courses I took in both my undergraduate degree in Marketing/Business Administration and my MBA degree, I still rank my undergraduate American Literature class as the one that had the biggest impact on me. Most especially, I liked the essays of Ralph Waldo Emerson, in particular, "Self-Reliance." I was lucky enough to be born in a country built on the concept of self-reliance versus government reliance.

When hiring new staff, the number one trait I look for in a potential employee is self-reliance.

Then there's the ultimate job as a parent, to present to the world a self-reliant and contributing individual.

Live in a Constant
State of Anticipation

One day, I accidentally happened upon the live televised service for Walter Payton, the great running back for the Chicago Bears. The minister delivering the eulogy noted, that right up to the day he died, Payton was anticipating what might happen next and was excited about what tomorrow might bring.

How perfect!, I thought to myself, to live your life in a constant state of anticipation. It keeps you alert, awake, and open to possibilities, no matter where you are in your life.

Mike and Marsha at a friend's wedding in 1968.

Get Ahead of Yourself

You may often hear the kind advice, "don't get out ahead of yourself." I have come to believe just the opposite, because I have seen positive results from getting out ahead of myself.

So, with faith in yourself and the ultimate outcome, stretch yourself. Set goals that force you reach beyond your comfort zone. You will be surprised how, like a rubber band, you snap ahead and catch up with yourself, both personally and professionally.

Great Opportunities Often Come in "the back door" not the front

You strive to obtain your objectives, your eyes fixed on the prize. I would suggest, however, that you also pay attention to what is happening behind you, coming in the back door. While I certainly work hard to reach the next milestone, sometimes the real opportunities have come knocking on the back door. Be alert!

Act like an "Owner" in your job

The person who thinks and acts like one of the owners of the company is the one who stands out. They don't just perform the tactical functions. They think strategically and help to take the organization to the next level.

The Power of the Questions you ask

I have read a few business books emphasizing this subject. One in particular, Spin Selling, did a great job of driving home this point. I have never stopped developing my ability to ask better questions. In the end, questions deepen your understanding about an issue, situation, or person. Certainly, you have to be a good listener, and great questions give you much more to listen for.

Under promise and over deliver

Integrity is your most critical asset, no matter your station in life. We work hard to protect it and build it. Yet, in the fight for a position, there is a strong temptation to overstate and overpromise, often for very sincere and well-meaning reasons. This only yields bad results. It tears away at your credibility, and ultimately diminishes your integrity.

Fight that temptation and opt for realistic expectations. It's a great feeling when you "surprise to the upside!"

Mike's official family portrait taken at their home in Powder Springs, GA. In 1994.

Finding/Eliminating "Bottlenecks" to maximize Productivity

In a book, The Goal, I learned the idea that you go only as fast as the place where you encounter a bottleneck allows you. The true rate of productivity in a factory was found at the bottleneck, the "pinch point." The concept applies to all sorts of life's activities, from business operations throughout society and into your personal life. I have been on a hunt to find bottlenecks ever since.

Let others do your cheerleading

In today's business world, you have to promote yourself. Learn to do it tactfully and strategically. People who only sing their own praises, recite their accomplishments, and put the spotlight on themselves are annoying. It also shows a total lack of class and maturity and actually diminishes their accomplishments.

Don't cheerlead for yourself, show humility as success can be fleeting. Pointing out your successes and showing admiration for what you've been able to achieve is best left to others. They will do a great job and you'll be seen as a person of class.

*Mike at his college graduation from
Northern Illinois University,
DeKalb, IL. , 1967*

Relationships -
The Dark Side of the Moon

I have come to understand that even the closest and most loving relationships may likely spend some time around the "dark side of the moon." There is nothing to be ashamed of, given that life brings many challenges that can overwhelm even the strongest of relationships.

Fortunately, for many, they do come out from behind that side of the moon and back into the bright sunlight of life. I am certain that those who do survive their time behind the dark side of the moon will be stronger for it. They will not only survive, they will thrive and succeed beyond their most positive expectations.

The Role of a Lifetime
You as a Role Model

Of the many musings about life and aging, the ones that stress that life and, most especially, aging "isn't for wimps" are the best. They are also very true. Yet, face life and aging we must and, hopefully, with class and grace.

A key for me has been the realization that my

*A more recent family photo of Mike's entire family
taken at their home in Lone Tree, CO*

children, and now my grandchildren, will get many of

their cues about living and aging from my example. My goal is to be a positive role model for them. As I have progressed through the decades, this has been a wonderful motivator for me and, without a doubt, it has made the challenges easier to accept and handle.

Again, let me say how grateful I am that you have chosen to "spend some time with me." I wish you, your family, your friends, and all of those you love my very best for a positive, productive, and lesson-filled life!

~*Mike Jaroch*

ACKNOWLEDGEMENTS

At the very time I decided to write my book, I was

fortunate to be introduced to Drew Ross by his brother Craig. Craig is a good friend and CEO of a Colorado-based leadership development company, Verus Global, that I've had the honor to work with.

Drew is a very accomplished writer and has made a significant contribution both in his support of my effort and the many suggestions and improvements he made to the text. Thank you so very much, Drew!

I was also fortunate to meet EJ Thornton and want to also thank her. EJ is a fellow author; but, more importantly for my project, she is also a publisher with particular expertise in putting one's work up on Amazon Kindle. The fast growing industry of eBooks is one I am excited to now be a part of thanks to EJ!

I look forward to continuing my collaboration with both EJ and Drew as we work together on a variety of marketing efforts on behalf of Extraordinary Lessons From An Ordinary Life.

ABOUT THE AUTHOR
MIKE JAROCH

How to explain someone's ability, from an early age, to pull the most meaningful lessons and truths about our lives from the ordinary occurrences of day-to-day life? Maybe as the third oldest of thirteen children the self-reliance required to move ahead and achieve caused such intense observation of events and interactions. In any case, Mike Jaroch, now at the age of 68, has documented all the key lessons and insights he has learned along the way. His two children, Julie and Michael, have blessed him and his wife, Marsha, with five grandsons. The guidance for those five boys was a primary motivation for Mike to capture these truths and the stories behind them. He hopes that they will serve many as they take on the challenges within their own lives.

Mike grew up in the small northern Illinois town of Mundelein. With a business degree from Northern Illinois University and a MBA from the Lake Forest

School of Management, he has enjoyed a very successful career with both large Fortune 50 companies and technology start-up ventures. For the past twelve years, he has been an independent management consultant working with a multitude of companies across a wide range of industries.

He and his wife now reside in Lone Tree, Colorado.

OTHER BOOKS
BY MIKE JAROCH

The Adventures
of the Sneeky Sneekers

The Tornado - *What would you do if some mysterious person gave you a gift with magical powers? Each of four brothers were given a gift of a pair of innocent looking sneakers, but the next thing anyone knows is one of the brothers is up in the top of a tree? What they discover about themselves and what they can do with their new-found powers takes them on an adventure of epic proportions! Not even Mother Nature's fury can stand up to the power of the Sneeky Sneekers!*

The Ghost of Gleason Mansion -*When Halloween is spoiled for The Sneeky Sneekers because of a spooky house some overly adventures and very careless children, something freaky and paranormal happens... and we're not just talking about the powers of the sneakers! Just who is the ghost of Gleason mansion and why does he need the help of The Sneeky Sneekers?*

Washout at Liberty Valley -*Four boys with special powers and an amazing secret are charged with 'only using their powers to help people.' But when three families ignore the sheriff's warnings to get out of harm's way, will the efforts of the Sneeky Sneekers be enough to save them from Mother Nature's fury and their own bad judgement?*

RECOMMENDED READING

Good to Great: Why Some Companies Make the Leap and others don't - *by Jim Collins* One of the absolute best business books of all time. A must read for college students on up to successful executives.

The Five Dysfunctions of a Team - *by Patrick Lencioni* It's all about the Team and this gem gives you the roadmap for how to make the Team as effective as possible. I have used it often in my coaching work with CEO's and their teams.

The New New Thing - *by Michael Lewis* A great read for all of those involved in Start-Up endeavors, whether high-tech or not.

Spin Selling - *by Neil Rackham* Everyone involved in Selling must read this book. Key takeaway is understanding the power of the questions you ask. Asking great questions is a key to success no matter what area of work you are involved with.

The Goal - *by Eliyahu M. Goldratt and Jeff Cox* Go to the Bottleneck in any process, operation to find the true rate of production and productivity. Become an expert at finding and correcting the bottlenecks.

Winning Through Intimidation - *by Robert J. Ringer* A classic in an important aspect of interpersonal relations. Yes, it may help you become more assertive; but, it also helps you see the intimidators coming and prepare for them accordingly.

A Good Walk Spoiled - *by John Feinstein* Every golfer can identify with this book. A great view inside the world of professional golf. Fun read.

blink - *by Malcolm Gladwell* Fortifies, with proof, the belief that trusting your own instincts may be one of the most important of all life's lessons.

The Autobiography of Calvin Coolidge - *by Calvin Coolidge* I had to learn more about the man who wrote my favorite quote and one of the most popular of all times - Persistence. His personal story in his own words is wonderful and revealing.

The Millionaire Next Door - *by Thomas J. Stanley and William D. Danko* A very interesting and well researched book about ordinary folks who have achieved financial well-being. Proof positive that it's your bottom line (net worth) that makes the difference in your true financial independence.

The Savage Truth on Money (2nd Edition) - *by Terry Savage* First came in contact with Terry Savage during our years in the Chicagoland area. When it comes to all the facts around money and money management, Terry has been my author of choice. She also has a great website.

Extraordinary Lessons
from an Ordinary Life
is available at
GreatMemoirs.com

RESOURCES

Ringer, Robert J. *Winning Through Intimidation* 1973, Self Published

Emerson, Ralph Waldo. *Self-Reliance* 1841, Essays First Series

Rackham, Neil. *Spin Selling* 1988, McGraw-Hill, Inc.

Goldratt, Dr. Eliyahu M. *The Goal* 1984, North River Press

IF YOU LIKED

EXTRAORDINARY LESSONS FROM AN ORDINARY LIFE

Please leave a review on

Amazon.com

Also available in Kindle

45251067R00051

Made in the USA
San Bernardino, CA
03 February 2017